LOW BUDGET MEAL PREP COOKBOOK

40 Tasty and Healthy Recipes to Make Nourishing Meals and Save Time

Robert Conroy

Copyright © 2023 by Robert Conroy.

All rights reserved.

No part of this publication may be reproduced, distributed, or transmitted in any form or by any means, including photocopying, recording, or other electronic or mechanical methods, without the prior written permission of the publisher, except in the case of brief quotations embodied in critical reviews and certain other noncommercial uses permitted by copyright law.

TABLE OF CONTENTS

INTRODUCTION

CHAPTER 1
Budget-Savvy Meal Planning

Smart Grocery Strategies

Seasonal and Sale Ingredient Utilization

CHAPTER 2
Cooking Economically and Flavorfully

Budget-Friendly Cooking Methods

Enhancing Taste with Affordable Ingredients

CHAPTER 3
Meal Prep Dishes

Breakfasts

Veggie Breakfast Burritos

Apple Cinnamon Chia Pudding

Overnight Oats

Egg Muffins

Peanut Butter Banana Toast

Greek Yogurt Parfait

Banana Pancakes

Rice Cake Delight

Breakfast Smoothie Packs

Breakfast Quinoa Bowl

Lunch

Chickpea Salad

Rice and Bean Burrito Bowl

Veggie Stir-Fry with Tofu

Quinoa and Roasted Vegetable Bowl

Pasta Salad

Lentil Soup

Peanut Butter and Jelly Sandwiches

Veggie Wrap

Egg Salad

Veggie Fried Rice

Minestrone Soup

Dinner Delights

Pasta Primavera

Potato Hash

Bean and Rice Burritos

Tuna Salad Wraps

Omelet with Veggies

Margherita Quesadillas

Spaghetti Aglio e Olio

Veggie and Cheese Quesadillas

Potato and Pea Curry

Peanut Butter Noodles

Tasty Snacks

Oven-Baked Sweet Potato Chips

Peanut Butter Energy Balls

Roasted Chickpeas

Veggie Sticks with Hummus

Sautéed Cinnamon Apple Slices

No-Bake Oat Bars

Trail Mix

Cucumber and Cottage Cheese Bites

Oven-Roasted Edamame

Homemade Granola Bars

Meal Plan

Day 1:

Day 2:

Day 3:

Day 4:

Day 5:

Day 6:

Day 7:

CONCLUSION

INTRODUCTION

Step into a world where delicious meets affordable – Welcome to the Low Budget Meal Prep Cookbook. In a small town, Sarah's culinary journey took a turn when she discovered this gem. As a busy single parent, she yearned for nutritious meals without breaking the bank.

Guided by the cookbook's practical approach, Sarah learned to navigate grocery aisles with purpose, picking budget-friendly ingredients while unlocking a world of flavors. With its easy-to-follow recipes and clever meal prep strategies, she transformed her kitchen into a hub of culinary ingenuity.

Weekends turned into a symphony of chopping, cooking, and organizing as Sarah prepped meals for the week. Soon, she realized the true power of the cookbook – not just saving money, but also crafting meals that spoke of care and creativity.

Welcome to a place where low budget doesn't mean low taste. The Low Budget Meal Prep Cookbook invites you to savor every bite of life without compromising on your wallet or your palate.

CHAPTER 1

Budget-Savvy Meal Planning

Creating cost-effective and delicious meals can be a challenging task, especially when working with a limited budget. Fortunately, there are smart grocery strategies and seasonal ingredient utilization techniques that can help you make the most out of your resources. In this section of the low budget meal prep cookbook, we'll delve into these strategies and offer insights on how to maximize your savings while still enjoying flavorful and nutritious meals.

Smart Grocery Strategies

1. Meal Planning: The foundation of any successful budget-friendly meal prep is effective meal planning. Sit down and create a weekly meal plan that outlines what you'll eat for breakfast, lunch, and dinner. You can avoid impulse buys and food waste by doing this.

2. Create a Shopping List: Based on your meal plan, create a thorough shopping list before you visit the grocery store. Stick to the list and avoid buying items that are not essential for your planned meals.
3. Buy in Bulk: Staples like rice, pasta, beans, and oats can be purchased in bulk, which often offers a lower cost per unit. Make sure you have enough room in your storage area to keep these products fresh.
4. Compare Prices: Don't hesitate to compare prices between different brands and stores. Sometimes, generic brands can be just as good as name brands at a fraction of the cost.

Seasonal and Sale Ingredient Utilization

1. Enjoy seasonal produce: Not only are seasonal fruits and vegetables more inexpensive, they are also fresher. Plan your meals around what's in season to take advantage of lower prices and better flavors.

2. Freeze and Preserve: When you come across a sale on ingredients like meat, poultry, or seafood, consider buying in bulk and freezing the excess. This way, you can extend their shelf life and save money in the long run.
3. Canned and Frozen Alternatives: Canned and frozen vegetables and fruits are often cheaper than fresh ones and can be just as nutritious. They also have a longer shelf life, reducing the risk of food spoilage.
4. Repurpose Leftovers: Get creative with leftovers to prevent food waste. For example, leftover roasted chicken can be turned into chicken salad for sandwiches, or excess cooked vegetables can be added to soups and stews.
5. Batch Cooking: Prepare larger quantities of meals and freeze individual portions for later consumption. This is not only a time-saver but also helps you avoid ordering takeout when you're short on time or ingredients.

6. DIY Sauces and Condiments: Instead of buying pre-packaged sauces and condiments, consider making your own. Basic ingredients like vinegar, oil, spices, and herbs can be combined to create flavorful dressings and sauces.

By combining these smart grocery strategies with the utilization of seasonal and sale ingredients, you'll be able to create a wide range of budget-friendly meals that are both satisfying and nutritious. With a little planning and creativity, you can master the art of meal prep while keeping your wallet happy.

CHAPTER 2

Cooking Economically and Flavorfully

Budget-Friendly Cooking Methods

1. Slow Cooking: Slow cookers are a budget-conscious chef's best friend. They transform tough cuts of meat and inexpensive ingredients into tender, flavorful meals. Just throw in your choice of protein, vegetables, and seasonings, and let it cook slowly for hours. This method not only develops rich flavors but also requires minimal effort.
2. One-Pot Meals: Embrace the convenience of one-pot cooking. By combining all your ingredients in a single pot or pan, you save on both cooking time and cleanup. Dishes like stews, casseroles, and stir-fries are perfect for this approach.
3. Roasting and Baking: Roasting and baking intensify flavors by caramelizing sugars and creating a golden crust. Use this method to enhance

the natural sweetness of vegetables, and to cook proteins like chicken, fish, and pork with minimal added fats.

4. Batch Cooking: Batch cooking involves preparing larger quantities of food at once and then portioning it out for multiple meals. This method saves time and energy, and it's an excellent way to reduce food waste by using up all your ingredients.

5. Grains and Legumes: Cooking grains and legumes like rice, quinoa, lentils, and beans is cost-effective and versatile. They can serve as the base for many dishes, providing protein and fiber to make your meals more satisfying.

Enhancing Taste with Affordable Ingredients

1. Herbs and Spices: Herbs and spices are budget-friendly ingredients that can transform your dishes. A pinch of dried herbs or a sprinkle of spices like cumin, paprika, and turmeric can elevate the taste of even the simplest meals.

2. Citrus Zest and Juice: Citrus fruits like lemons, limes, and oranges are affordable sources of flavor. Zest adds a burst of aromatic essence, while a squeeze of juice brightens up your dishes.
3. Onions and Garlic: Onions and garlic are foundational ingredients in many cuisines. They're inexpensive, add depth to your dishes, and can be sautéed as a base for soups, stews, and sauces.
4. Stock and Broth: Making your own vegetable or chicken stock from kitchen scraps and bones is not only environmentally friendly but also cost-effective. Stocks enhance the depth of flavors in soups, sauces, and rice dishes.
5. Affordable Cuts of Meat: Instead of splurging on expensive cuts of meat, opt for economical options like chicken thighs, ground meat, or tougher cuts suitable for slow cooking. With the right cooking method and seasonings, these cuts can be just as delicious.
6. Texture and Crunch: Adding texture to your dishes can make them more enjoyable. Ingredients like

toasted nuts, seeds, and breadcrumbs can be used as toppings to provide a satisfying crunch.

7. Creative Use of Leftovers: Turn yesterday's meal into today's masterpiece. Leftover roasted vegetables can be blended into soups, and yesterday's cooked rice can be transformed into flavorful fried rice with a few simple additions.

By utilizing these budget-friendly cooking methods and enhancing taste with affordable ingredients, you'll be able to create a diverse array of mouthwatering dishes that don't strain your finances. Experiment with different combinations and techniques to discover a world of flavors that won't compromise your budget.

CHAPTER 3

Meal Prep Dishes

Breakfasts

Veggie Breakfast Burritos

Ingredients

- Whole wheat tortillas
- Scrambled eggs
- Sautéed vegetables (onions, bell peppers, etc.)
- Salsa or hot sauce

Method:

1. Lay out tortillas and add scrambled eggs and sautéed vegetables.
2. Add salsa or hot sauce for flavor.
3. Roll up the tortillas, tuck in the sides, and wrap in foil for easy reheating.

Apple Cinnamon Chia Pudding

Ingredients:

- 3 tablespoons chia seeds
- 1 cup milk (dairy or plant-based)
- 1 apple, grated
- ½ teaspoon cinnamon
- Nuts for topping

Method:

1. Mix chia seeds, milk, grated apple, and cinnamon in a container.
2. Refrigerate for a few hours or overnight, stirring occasionally.
3. Top with nuts before serving.

Overnight Oats

Ingredients:

- 1 cup rolled oats
- 1 cup milk (dairy or plant-based)
- 1 tablespoon honey or maple syrup

- Fresh fruits or nuts for topping

Method:

- In a jar, combine oats, milk, and sweetener.
- Stir well and refrigerate overnight.
- Before serving, add your favorite toppings.

Egg Muffins

Ingredients:

- 6 eggs
- ½ cup diced vegetables (bell peppers, spinach, etc.)
- ¼ cup shredded cheese
- Salt and pepper to taste

Method:

- Preheat the oven to 350°F (175°C) and grease a muffin tin.
- In a bowl, whisk eggs and add vegetables, cheese, salt, and pepper.
- Pour the mixture into muffin cups and bake for about 20-25 minutes.

Peanut Butter Banana Toast

Ingredients:

- Whole wheat bread slices
- Peanut butter
- Sliced bananas
- Honey (optional)

Method:

1. Toast the bread slices.
2. Spread peanut butter on each slice.
3. If preferred, add slices of banana and an additional drizzle of honey on the top.

Greek Yogurt Parfait

Ingredients:

- Greek yogurt
- Granola
- Mixed berries
- Honey

Method:

1. In a jar or container, layer granola, Greek yogurt, and berries.
2. Drizzle with honey and repeat the layers.
3. Refrigerate and enjoy.

Banana Pancakes

Ingredients:

- 2 ripe bananas, mashed
- 2 eggs
- ½ teaspoon vanilla extract
- ½ cup rolled oats

Method:

- Mix mashed bananas, eggs, and vanilla extract.
- Add rolled oats and stir well.
- Cook spoonful of batter on a griddle until golden brown on both sides.

Rice Cake Delight

Ingredients:

- Rice cakes

- Cottage cheese or cream cheese
- Sliced tomatoes or cucumber
- Sprouts or herbs

Method:

1. Spread cottage cheese or cream cheese on rice cakes.
2. Top with sliced tomatoes or cucumber and sprouts.
3. Season with salt and pepper.

Breakfast Smoothie Packs

Ingredients (for each pack):

- Frozen fruits (berries, banana, etc.)
- Spinach or kale
- Protein powder (optional)
- Almond milk or water

Method:

1. Prepare individual bags with frozen fruits and greens.

2. In the morning, blend with protein powder and liquid until smooth.

Breakfast Quinoa Bowl

Ingredients:

- Cooked quinoa
- Sliced almonds
- Dried fruits (raisins, cranberries, etc.)
- Milk or yogurt

Method:

1. In a bowl, mix cooked quinoa, sliced almonds, and dried fruits.
2. Add milk or yogurt and stir.

Lunch

Chickpea Salad

Ingredients:

- 1 can of chickpeas, drained and rinsed
- Diced vegetables (cucumber, bell peppers, red onion, etc.)

- Chopped fresh herbs (parsley, cilantro)
- Lemon juice and olive oil for dressing

Method:

1. Combine chickpeas, diced vegetables, and herbs in a bowl.
2. Drizzle with lemon juice and olive oil, and mix well.
3. Divide into containers for meal prepping.

Rice and Bean Burrito Bowl

Ingredients:

- Cooked rice
- Canned black beans or pinto beans
- Sautéed vegetables (bell peppers, onions, corn)
- Salsa or guacamole

Method:

1. Assemble bowls with rice, beans, sautéed vegetables, and toppings.

2. Store salsa or guacamole separately to prevent sogginess.

Veggie Stir-Fry with Tofu

Ingredients:

- Tofu, cubed
- Assorted stir-fry vegetables (broccoli, carrots, snap peas, etc.)
- Stir-fry sauce (soy sauce, ginger, garlic, etc.)

Method:

1. Sauté tofu until lightly browned, then set aside.
2. Stir-fry vegetables in a hot pan, adding tofu back in.
3. Add stir-fry sauce and cook until heated through.
4. Pack with cooked rice or noodles.

Quinoa and Roasted Vegetable Bowl

Ingredients:

- Cooked quinoa

- Roasted vegetables (zucchini, eggplant, carrots, etc.)
- Feta cheese or nuts (optional)
- Balsamic vinaigrette

Method:

1. Mix quinoa with roasted vegetables and cheese or nuts.
2. Drizzle with balsamic vinaigrette before serving.

Pasta Salad

Ingredients:

- Cooked pasta (penne, fusilli, etc.)
- Chopped vegetables (tomatoes, cucumbers, olives, etc.)
- Italian dressing

Method:

1. Toss cooked pasta with chopped vegetables and dressing.
2. Refrigerate and enjoy cold.

Lentil Soup

Ingredients:

- Red or green lentils
- Chopped onions, carrots, celery
- Vegetable broth or water
- Spices (cumin, paprika, etc.)

Method:

1. Sauté onions, carrots, and celery until softened.
2. Add lentils, spices, and broth or water.
3. Simmer until lentils are cooked through.
4. Divide into portions for meal prep.

Peanut Butter and Jelly Sandwiches

Ingredients:

- Whole wheat bread
- Peanut butter
- Fruit preserves or jelly

Method:

1. On one slice of bread, spread with peanut butter.
2. Spread fruit preserves or jelly on another slice.
3. Press slices together to make a sandwich.

Veggie Wrap

Ingredients:

- Whole wheat tortillas
- Hummus or cream cheese
- Sliced vegetables (cucumber, bell peppers, etc.)
- Spinach or lettuce

Method:

1. Spread hummus or cream cheese on tortillas.
2. Add sliced vegetables and greens.
3. Roll up tightly and wrap in foil or parchment paper.

Egg Salad

Ingredients:

- Hard-boiled eggs, chopped
- Chopped celery and onions

- Mayonnaise or Greek yogurt
- Mustard (optional)
- Salt and pepper

Method:

1. Mix chopped eggs, celery, and onions in a bowl.
2. Add mayonnaise or Greek yogurt, and mustard if desired.
3. Season with salt and pepper.
4. Serve on whole wheat bread or with crackers.

Veggie Fried Rice

Ingredients:

- Cooked rice (preferably day-old)
- Mixed vegetables (peas, carrots, corn, etc.)
- Eggs (optional)
- Soy sauce
- Sesame oil
- Scallions (chopped)

Method:

1. Heat a pan and add mixed vegetables. Cook until tender.
2. Push vegetables to the side and scramble eggs if using.
3. Add cooked rice to the pan and stir-fry with vegetables and eggs.
4. Mix thoroughly after drizzling with soy sauce and sesame oil.
5. Garnish with chopped scallions.

Minestrone Soup

Ingredients:

- Mixed vegetables (carrots, celery, zucchini, etc.)
- Canned diced tomatoes
- Canned beans (kidney beans, cannellini beans, etc.)
- Vegetable broth
- Pasta or rice
- Italian herbs (oregano, basil, thyme)
- Salt and pepper

Method:

1. Sauté mixed vegetables until slightly softened.
2. Add canned tomatoes, beans, and vegetable broth.
3. Season with Italian herbs, salt, and pepper.
4. Simmer until vegetables are tender and flavors meld.

Dinner Delights

Pasta Primavera

Ingredients:

- Pasta of your choice
- Assorted vegetables (zucchini, cherry tomatoes, peas)
- 2 tablespoons olive oil
- Grated Parmesan cheese

Method:

1. Cook the pasta according to package directions, then drain and put aside.
2. Heat the olive oil in a large pan over medium heat.
3. Sauté the veggies until they are soft and slightly browned.

4. Toss in the cooked pasta and mix well, letting the flavors combine.
5. Serve the pasta primavera with a sprinkle of grated Parmesan cheese.

Potato Hash

Ingredients:

- 2-3 potatoes (diced)
- 1 onion (chopped)
- 1 bell pepper (chopped)
- 2 tablespoons cooking oil
- 1 teaspoon paprika
- 1 teaspoon thyme

Method:

1. In a pan, heat the cooking oil over medium-low heat.
2. Add the diced potatoes and cook until they're crispy and golden brown.
3. Add the chopped onion and bell pepper to the skillet and sauté until they're tender.

4. Sprinkle the paprika and thyme over the mixture and stir to combine.
5. Serve the potato hash as a delicious side dish.

Bean and Rice Burritos

Ingredients:

- Cooked rice
- Canned black beans (drained and rinsed)
- 1 onion (chopped)
- 1 bell pepper (chopped)
- 1 teaspoon chili powder
- Flour tortillas
- Sour cream and salsa (for serving)

Method:

1. In a pan, sauté the chopped onion and bell pepper until softened.
2. Add the drained black beans and chili powder, cooking until heated through.
3. Warm the flour tortillas, then spoon rice and bean mixture onto each one.

4. Roll up the tortillas to form burritos.
5. Serve with a dollop of sour cream and salsa.

Tuna Salad Wraps

Ingredients:

- 1 can of tuna (drained)
- ¼ cup Greek yogurt (or mayo)
- 1 celery stalk (chopped)
- ¼ onion (chopped)
- Lettuce leaves
- 4 whole-wheat wraps

Method:

1. In a bowl, mix the drained tuna, Greek yogurt, chopped celery, and onion.
2. Lay out the whole-wheat wraps and place lettuce leaves on them.
3. Spoon the tuna mixture onto the lettuce and wrap it up.

Omelet with Veggies

Ingredients:

- 3 eggs
- Handful of spinach leaves
- 1 tomato (chopped)
- 3-4 mushrooms (sliced)
- Grated cheese (optional)
- Salt and pepper to taste

Method:

1. Add salt and pepper to the eggs after whisking them in a bowl.
2. In a skillet with a little oil, add the sliced mushrooms. Cook until they're soft and slightly browned.
3. Add the chopped tomato and spinach leaves to the pan, cooking until the spinach wilts.
4. Over the vegetables, pour the whisked eggs, and cook until set. If desired, sprinkle grated cheese on one half of the omelet before folding it over.

Margherita Quesadillas

Ingredients:

- 4 flour tortillas
- 1 tomato (sliced)
- Fresh mozzarella cheese (sliced)
- Fresh basil leaves
- Olive oil
- Salt and pepper to taste

Method:

1. Lay out a tortilla and place slices of mozzarella, tomato, and basil leaves on one half.
2. Season with salt and pepper and fold the tortilla in half.
3. In a pan, heat a little amount of olive oil over medium heat.
4. Cook the quesadilla on both sides until the cheese has melted and the tortilla is crisp and golden.
5. Repeat for the remaining tortillas.

Spaghetti Aglio e Olio

Ingredients:

- Spaghetti
- 4 cloves garlic (thinly sliced)
- Red pepper flakes (to taste)
- Olive oil
- Fresh parsley (chopped)
- Grated Parmesan cheese

Method:

1. Cook the spaghetti according to the package instructions; drain and set aside.
2. In a pan, heat olive oil over low heat and add the sliced garlic and red pepper flakes. Cook the garlic until it is golden but not burnt.
3. Cooked spaghetti is tossed in garlic-flavored oil.
4. Before serving, top with grated Parmesan cheese and chopped parsley.

Veggie and Cheese Quesadillas

Ingredients:

- Flour tortillas
- Mixed vegetables (bell peppers, onions, zucchini)
- Grated cheese (cheddar, mozzarella)
- Cooking oil

Method:

1. In a pan, heat a little oil over medium heat.
2. Add the chopped mixed vegetables and sauté until tender.
3. Place a tortilla in the pan, sprinkle grated cheese on one half, then top with sautéed vegetables and more cheese.
4. Fold the tortilla in half and cook until both sides are golden and the cheese is melted.
5. Serve wedge-cut with salsa or sour cream.

Potato and Pea Curry

Ingredients:

- Potatoes (cubed)
- 1 cup frozen peas
- Onion (chopped)
- 2 cloves garlic (minced)
- Curry spices (turmeric, cumin, coriander, garam masala)
- Canned diced tomatoes
- Cooking oil
- Fresh cilantro (chopped)

Method:

1. Heat oil in a pan and sauté the chopped onion until soft.
2. Cook for another minute after adding the minced garlic.
3. Add the cubed potatoes and sauté until they start to brown.

4. Stir in the curry spices and cook for a minute until fragrant.
5. Add the canned tomatoes and a little water, then cover and simmer until the potatoes are tender.
6. Simmer for a few more minutes after adding the frozen peas.
7. Garnish with chopped cilantro before serving.

Peanut Butter Noodles

Ingredients:

- Noodles of your choice
- ¼ cup peanut butter
- Soy sauce
- 1 tablespoon sesame oil
- 1 teaspoon ginger (minced)
- Crushed peanuts (optional)
- Green onions (chopped)

Method:

1. Noodles should be prepared as directed on the package; drain and set aside

2. In a bowl, mix peanut butter, soy sauce, sesame oil, and minced ginger to create a sauce.
3. Toss the cooked noodles in the peanut sauce until well coated.
4. Serve the peanut butter noodles garnished with chopped green onions and crushed peanuts.

Tasty Snacks

Oven-Baked Sweet Potato Chips

- **Ingredients:**
  Sweet potatoes
- Olive oil
- Salt, optional spices.

Method:

1. Slice sweet potatoes into thin rounds.
2. Toss with olive oil, salt, and any desired spices.
3. Arrange on a baking sheet and bake at 375°F (190°C) for 15-20 minutes, flipping halfway through.

Peanut Butter Energy Balls

Ingredients:

- Oats
- Peanut butter
- Honey, optional add-ins (chocolate chips, dried fruits).

Method:

- In a bowl, combine oats, peanut butter, honey, and any add-ins.
- Roll into small balls and refrigerate for at least 30 minutes before serving.

Roasted Chickpeas

Ingredients:

- Canned chickpeas,
- Olive oil
- Salt, spices of your choice.

Method:

1. Drain and rinse chickpeas before patting them dry.

2. Toss with olive oil, salt, and spices.
3. Spread on a baking sheet and bake at 400°F (200°C) for 20-30 minutes, until crispy.

Veggie Sticks with Hummus

Ingredients:

- Carrots
- Cucumbers
- Bell peppers (or any desired veggies)
- Hummus (homemade or store-bought).

Method:

1. Slice veggies like carrots, cucumbers, and bell peppers into sticks.
2. Serve with hummus for dipping.

Sautéed Cinnamon Apple Slices

Ingredients:

- Apples
- Butter or coconut oil
- Cinnamon

Method:

1. Slice apples and sauté in a pan with a little butter or coconut oil.
2. Sprinkle with cinnamon and cook until tender.

No-Bake Oat Bars

Ingredients:

- Rolled oats
- Peanut butter
- Honey
- Mix-ins (dried fruits, chocolate chips, nuts)

Method:

1. Mix rolled oats, peanut butter, and honey in a bowl.
2. Add your choice of mix-ins and press into a pan.
3. Chill in the refrigerator, then cut into bars.

Trail Mix

Ingredients:

- Nuts, seeds
- Dried fruits

- Dark chocolate chips

Method:

1. Choose your favorite dried fruit, nut, seed, and chocolate chip combinations.
2. Store in individual snack-sized bags for a quick on-the-go snack.

Cucumber and Cottage Cheese Bites

Ingredients:

- Cucumber
- Cottage cheese
- Salt, pepper
- Herbs (dill, parsley).

Method:

1. Slice cucumber into rounds and top each with a dollop of cottage cheese.
2. Season with salt, pepper, and herbs.

Oven-Roasted Edamame

Ingredients:

- Frozen edamame
- Olive oil
- Salt, optional spices.

Method:

1. Toss frozen edamame with olive oil, salt, and spices like garlic powder or chili powder.
2. Spread on a baking sheet and bake at 400°F (200°C) for 15-20 minutes, until lightly crispy.

Homemade Granola Bars

Ingredients:

- Rolled oats
- Honey, nut butter
- Dried fruits, nuts
- Chocolate chips

Method:

1. In a mixing bowl, combine rolled oats, honey, nut butter, and mix-ins like dried fruits, nuts, or chocolate chips.
2. Place the mixture in a baking dish and place in the refrigerator until hard.
3. Cut into bars and keep in an airtight container.

Meal Plan

Day 1:

Breakfast: Apple Cinnamon Chia Pudding

Lunch: Rice and Bean Burrito Bowl

Snacks: Oven-Baked Sweet Potato Chips

Dinner: Margherita Quesadillas

Day 2:

Breakfast: Peanut Butter Banana Toast

Lunch: Pasta Salad

Snacks: Roasted Chickpeas

Dinner: Potato and Pea Curry

Day 3:

Breakfast: Breakfast Smoothie Packs

Lunch: Minestrone Soup

Snacks: Cucumber and Cottage Cheese Bites

Dinner: Spaghetti Aglio e Olio

Day 4:

Breakfast: Veggie Breakfast Burritos

Lunch: Quinoa and Roasted Vegetable Bowl

Snacks: Peanut Butter Energy Balls

Dinner: Tuna Salad Wraps

Day 5:

Breakfast: Egg Muffins

Lunch: Veggie Stir-Fry with Tofu

Snacks: Sautéed Cinnamon Apple Slices

Dinner: Omelet with Veggies

Day 6:

Breakfast: Quinoa Bowl

Lunch: Lentil Soup

Snacks: Trail Mix

Dinner: Pasta Primavera

Day 7:

Breakfast: Banana Pancakes

Lunch: Veggie Wrap

Snacks: Oven-Roasted Edamame

Dinner: Veggie and Cheese Quesadillas

CONCLUSION

In a world where busy schedules and financial constraints often challenge our ability to eat healthily, this cookbook aims to empower you with the knowledge and inspiration needed to create delicious and satisfying meals without breaking the bank.

Through the journey of these recipes, we've explored a myriad of flavors, textures, and culinary possibilities that prove that eating on a budget doesn't mean sacrificing taste or nutrition.

Meal prepping isn't just about saving money; it's about investing in your well-being. The recipes shared in this book are a testament to the fact that with a little creativity and planning, you can whip up meals that are not only easy on the wallet but also nourishing for your body and soul.

From hearty breakfasts to delightful lunches and tempting snacks, each recipe has been carefully crafted to provide you with a balanced and budget-friendly culinary experience.

As you embark on your meal prepping journey, remember that you hold the power to take control of your food choices and make a positive impact on your health and financial goals.

By planning ahead, utilizing budget-friendly ingredients, and making the most of your time in the kitchen, you're laying the foundation for a lifestyle that values both your physical well-being and your financial stability.

I hope that this cookbook has served as a trusted companion, guiding you through the process of creating flavorful and wholesome meals that fit seamlessly into your budget-conscious lifestyle.

May your kitchen be filled with the aroma of success and the joy of culinary exploration, and may your plate always be a canvas for your creativity and good taste.

Bon appétit!

Made in the USA
Columbia, SC
22 May 2024